Contents

Some words are shown in
bold letters, **like this**. You can
find out what these words mean
by looking in the Glossary.

Introduction

You are about to go on an amazing journey. You are going to follow in the footsteps of the great explorers to discover two of the coldest, wildest and most **isolated** places on Earth. You are going to travel to the Arctic and Antarctic.

You will travel up from the very depths of the freezing ocean, up onto **permanently** frozen lands covered in thick ice. You will discover how each part of the sea and land is home to amazing animals and plants. Each has its own special way to survive in these hard and hostile conditions at the ends of our Earth.

The Antarctic, and areas of the Arctic, are permanently frozen and covered with ice.

The Arctic is actually a huge frozen ocean around the **North Pole**. Antarctica is an enormous **continent** around the **South Pole**. When it is winter in the Arctic, it is summer in the Antarctic. When it is winter in the Antarctic, it is summer in the Arctic. During the long winter months there are blizzards and freezing temperatures. Average winter temperatures are −30°C in the Arctic and −60°C in the Antarctic. There is constant darkness because the Sun is shining at the other pole. When summer comes, the Sun's rays melt some of the ice and snow. Many animals **migrate** to the area in the summer to feed, breed and rear their young.

As the Earth turns round the Sun, the pole facing towards the Sun will have its summer months whilst the other pole is in winter darkness.

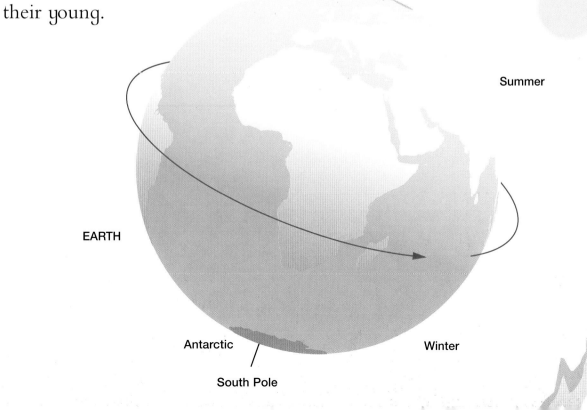

North Pole

Arctic

SUN

Summer

EARTH

Antarctic

South Pole

Winter

Journey map

Here are two maps showing the polar regions we are going to explore. We are going to start in a **submersible**, deep under the sea. We are going to rise up to the surface and walk onto the ice-sheet above it. We will then travel by **skidoo** across the ice.

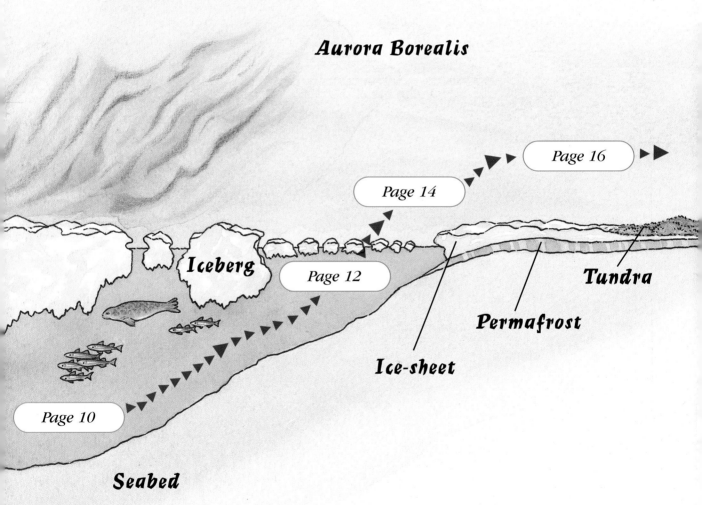

Aurora Borealis

Page 16

Page 14

Page 12

Iceberg

Tundra

Permafrost

Ice-sheet

Page 10

Seabed

ARCTIC

The poles are made up of layers of frozen ice. Some parts of these ice-sheets are thought to be 200,000 years old. As more and more snow pushes down onto this ice, some of the ice may begin to move slowly downwards towards the sea. This is called a **glacier**. Wind and waves break some of this ice off and it floats in the water as huge **icebergs**.

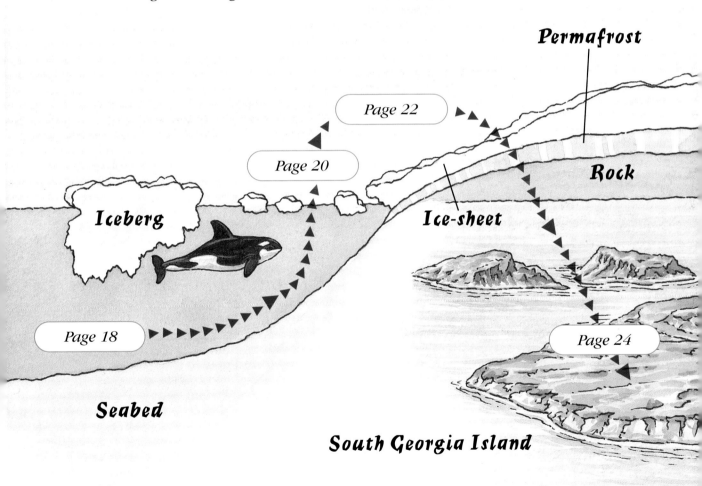

Permafrost

Page 22

Page 20

Rock

Iceberg

Ice-sheet

Page 18

Page 24

Seabed

South Georgia Island

ANTARCTIC

THE ARCTIC
Up from the depths

Our journey begins in a **submersible** on the seabed of the Arctic Ocean. It is cold and dark. We can hardly see anything through our **portholes** until something swims right past. Beneath us on the seabed are brittle starfish and sea-urchins, living amidst the broken-down remains of dead animals and dead **plankton**. We hope to catch a glance of a sperm whale. All whales are **mammals**, and have to come to the surface of the sea to breathe, but sperm whales can hold their breath and dive as deep as 1000 metres! Here in the icy ocean depths they fight huge battles with their prey, giant squid. The battles can leave the whales covered in scars, made by squid suckers.

Sperm whales have an enormous and strange-looking **snout**. It is full of liquid wax, called spermaceti oil, which helps the whales to sink down into the depths to hunt.

Beluga whale

The beluga, or white whale, is one of the few animals that can live in the cold of the Arctic Ocean all year round. Most beluga choose to come here in the summer only, when they can feast on the polar cod, haddock and other fish.

Narwhal

The narwhal, like the beluga and sperm whale, is a toothed whale that lives in a **pod**. The whales in the pod 'talk' to each other by making whistles and clicks through their blowholes.

Giant squid

Giant squid are huge and mysterious creatures that live deep down towards the bottom of the ocean. No one has ever seen one alive, but remains have been found on beaches.

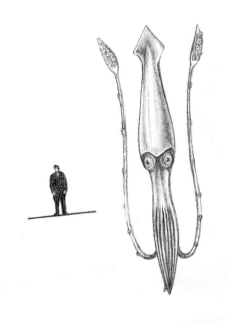

At the pack-ice

As we reach the surface and the edge of the **pack-ice** shelf, we open the hatch on top of the **submersible**. The air is icy and fresh. We can see and hear a wealth of animal life around us, making the most of the Arctic summer. Although it is summer, it is very cold here and we are surrounded by ice. The ice floating on top of the sea is only a few metres thick, but dotted around us are massive **icebergs**. Icebergs are chunks of ice that have broken off the main ice-sheet and floated away. They will gradually break up and melt, but this can take two to three years. Big icebergs can be dangerous to ships. Only a small part of the iceberg shows at the surface of the sea – most is hidden underwater.

The moving **glacier** has made a platform of ice in the sea that is still joined to the land.

1 little auk
2 harp seal
3 eider duck
4 ringed seal
5 ringed seal lair
6 walrus
7 plankton
8 puffins
9 iceberg
10 glacier

Ringed seal

The female uses her teeth and flippers to scrape funnel-shaped tunnels through the ice to breathing holes at the surface. She will give birth to her pups in the safety and warmth of her **lair**.

Plankton →

Plankton are tiny plants and animals that can be found in all seas. They float near the surface of the sea, soaking up the sun's rays, which help them to grow. Plankton are very important because they are food for many animals, both large and small.

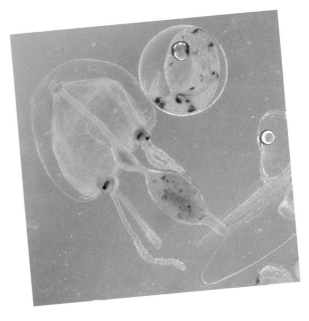

Walrus

Walruses spend their time hunting in the sea or resting on the ice. They have **tusks** that can be up to 90 cm long. They use them to dig up clams and shellfish from the seabed.

On the ice-sheet

It is time to leave the **submersible** and jump down onto the main ice-sheet. Although it is night time now, the Sun has not set. There is something strange above us. The sky is full of bright trails of brilliant light. These are the northern lights, or *Aurora Borealis*. They form when energy from the Sun's rays mixes with gases in the Earth's atmosphere above the **North Pole**. They make the gases give off wispy trails of coloured light.

Be careful and stand very still! Something else has been drawn to the lights. Prowling quietly ahead of us is the King of the Arctic – the polar bear. Once it has passed by, we must escape by **skidoo** and speed inland, over the ice, to the **tundra**.

During the Arctic winter months the Sun never rises, and in the summer months the Sun never sets. The area is sometimes called the land of the midnight Sun.

Ptarmigan

This hardy bird lives in the Arctic all year round. It is white in winter, so it blends in with the ice and is hidden from its **prey** and from **predators**. In the summer its feathers change to a brownish colour.

Polar bear

This is the largest bear in the world. The male is almost twice as tall as the average human male and ten times as heavy. They have good eyesight, a very sensitive sense of smell and sharp claws, all of which help them to hunt.

White hunter

Polar bears eat birds, fish and plants, but their favourite food is ringed seal. A bear will lie quietly next to a seal's breathing hole for hours, covering its black nose with its white paw. When the seal pops its head out of the hole, the bear grabs it and kills it with its paws and teeth.

Across the tundra

We have reached the **tundra**, the area of Arctic land that is exposed during the brief summer **thaw**. The ground is covered with wet and boggy soil. A little below the surface is a frozen layer called **permafrost**.

The temperature has risen, but only to 7°C! This is enough for mosses, lichen and small bushes to blossom. Insects have emerged from their winter sleep. Huge herds of animals have **migrated** here to enjoy a feeding and breeding season that will last for six to eight weeks, or until the summer ends. It is time to plan our next amazing journey south to experience what life is like in summer in the Antarctic.

1 mosquitoes
2 skuas
3 butterflies
4 grizzly bear
5 grey wolf
6 musk oxen
7 snow geese
8 caribou
9 snowshoe hare
10 arctic fox
11 moose
12 arctic willow
13 northern fleabane
14 golden eagle
15 reindeer moss
16 snowy owl
17 lemmings
18 mosses and lichens

In summer thousands of animals migrate to the Arctic tundra.

Caribou

Caribou are a type of deer known as reindeer in Europe and Asia. In summer thousands of them trek north over familiar routes, from forests on the edge of the Arctic, up to their summer breeding ground in the tundra.

Northern fleabane ⟶

This plant flowers during the Arctic summer. Fleas and midges hate its taste, which is how it got its name. Humans can use it as an insect repellent.

Lemmings

Lemmings are **rodents** that spend a lot of their lives sheltering in burrows under the ground. If they come out into the open in summer, larger animals like the snowy owl or golden eagle hunt and eat them.

THE ANTARCTIC
Deep-sea approach

We have completed our long journey to Antarctica and are now resting on the seabed in a **submersible**. We begin the long journey to the surface. As the dark water begins to get lighter we realise that there is an amazing amount of sea-life down here. The animals at the bottom feed on each other, or on dead **plankton** that falls from the surface. As we rise up into the mid-water we see huge **shoals** of fish. There is plenty of food for fish-eating **predators** like penguins and seals. The penguins and seals provide food for even larger Antarctic predators like leopard seals and orca. The orca hunt in packs of up to twelve and are usually led by a large male.

1 anemones
2 sponges
3 starfish
4 sea-spider
5 sea-urchin
6 orca
7 cod
8 ross seal
9 krill

The Antarctic is rich in sea-life.

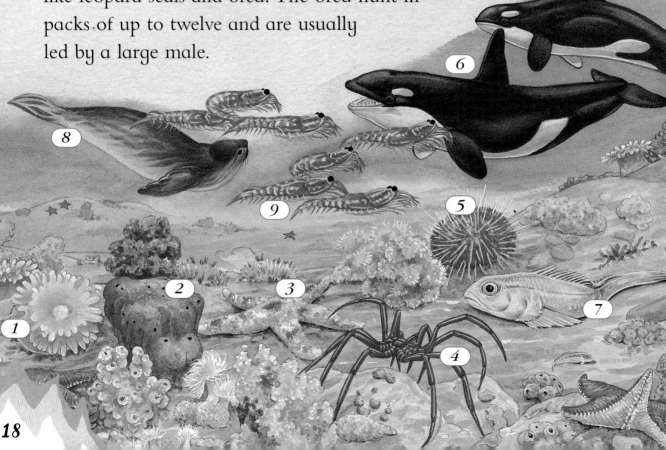

18

Sponge

There are approximately 300 varieties of sponge in the Antarctic Ocean. Some of them can live for several hundred years.

Starfish

Antarctic starfish are bright red. They have special feet like tubes with which they grasp their **prey**, once they have located it by smell. Antarctic starfish can live for many years on the seabed.

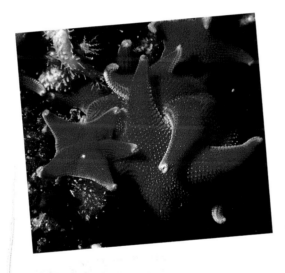

Sea-anemones

Sea-anemones look like blobs of jelly, but they have strong and deadly **tentacles** with which they can catch their prey, such as small fish or starfish. They use their tentacles to push the prey into their mouth opening.

At the sea's edge

As we reach the sea's surface and the edge of the land, the first thing that strikes us is the number of seals! There are millions of them breeding in **colonies** all along the ice-covered coast. There are weddell seals, which can dive for over an hour hunting for fish. There are ross seals, silver-coated crabeater seals and ferocious leopard seals. We see some elephant seals, including some gigantic fighting males. These elephant seals were hunted almost to **extinction** in the nineteenth century. The largest group of all is the crabeaters. This is a safe breeding ground for most of them with plenty of food in the sea. There can be up to 30 million of them living in the sea, or on the floating ice-blocks!

Vast colonies of seals and penguins live on the Antarctic **pack ice**.

1. icefish
2. antarctic cod
3. albatross
4. ross seal
5. leopard seal
6. crabeater seal
7. weddel seal
8. adelie penguins
9. elephant seal

Antarctic icefish

The Antarctic icefish is sometimes called the antifreeze fish because it has special antifreeze **molecules** in its body. These stop its blood and other fluids from freezing in the icy Antarctic seas.

Krill ⟶

Krill are small, shrimp-like creatures that are about 5cm long. In winter, they live under the pack-ice eating algae and **plankton**. In summer they swim together in huge groups and are food for the whales, penguins and seals.

Leopard seal

Leopard seals are terrifying **predators**. They hunt fish, penguins and other seals. Sometimes they creep up on a penguin underneath the ice, then smash up through the ice to catch it.

On the ice-sheet

At last we have reached the Antarctic ice-sheet, the coldest place on Earth. Many animals battle for food here. It is very noisy and very cold. We are surrounded on all sides by penguins, the most famous residents of the **Southern Hemisphere**.

Penguins are birds that cannot fly, but their wings and streamlined shape make them excellent swimmers. They can stay underwater for up to eighteen minutes, steering with their feet and swimming with their strong wings. They catch fish, squid and krill to eat. In the summer they come ashore to their nesting sites to lay their eggs and feed their young.

One parent stays with the egg while the other goes to sea to feed. At three weeks the chicks join crèches of other chicks. The babies stay together, while the adults search for food for them.

The most common Antarctic penguin is the adelie penguin.

Arctic tern

The Arctic tern breeds in the **Northern Hemisphere** in the summer, then **migrates** to the Antarctic in the Southern Hemisphere.

Emperor penguin

The female lays a single egg in autumn, which she gives to the male to look after. He keeps it warm in a pouch above his feet. The males huddle together, while the females go to sea to feed. They may not return for two months. The males wait with the chicks in the winter darkness, while the worst storms in the world crash around them, without food until the females return.

Skua

Skuas are large aggressive gulls with sharp, hooked beaks. They nest near penguin **colonies** so that they can steal and eat penguin chicks and eggs.

Antarctic islands

We are now at the final stage of our journey. We have crossed the sea to one of the islands off the coast of Antarctica. During the summer, islands like South Georgia are green and mostly free of snow. The island's small lakes have **thawed** a little and will remain thawed for a month or two. Every year, about 300,000 seals come here to find food and breed. As we reach the beaches, we can see thousands of these seals. The noise is deafening.

As the winter draws nearer, even these animals will begin to **migrate** to warmer places. Here, we too must end our amazing journey.

South Georgia is an island slightly north of the **pack-ice** of Antarctica.

24

Elephant seals

The elephant seal is the largest seal in the world and can reach up to 6m in length. The males have big trunk-like noses. They fight great battles to decide which will **mate** with the smaller females.

Albatross ⟶

The wandering albatross has the biggest wingspan of all birds – as much as 3.63m! It uses its huge wings to catch the strong sea winds and let them carry it at speeds of 80km per hour!

Nesting giants

Thousands of albatross breed on South Georgia Island. The adults find food for the chicks. When they return to the nest the chick taps on the adult's beak. This instantly makes the adult **regurgitate** the food for the chick to eat.

Conservation and the future

At risk

As our plane takes off from Antarctica, we see the spectacular **continent** lying below us, almost untouched by human existence. However, both the Arctic and Antarctic are at risk from human pollution and hunting, and must be protected if the animal and plant life there is to continue to **thrive**.

Many species of animals have been hunted over the years for their skins. Animals like polar bears, musk oxen, seals and whales have faced **extinction**. Most are now protected. Fishing limits have also been set to prevent vast numbers of krill, squid and other fish from being caught, damaging the **food chain**.

The 1989 Exxon Valdez oil spill off Alaska polluted sea-life in the Arctic area.

Pollution

Pollution has also harmed life at the poles. Pollution from oil spills, **radiation** from nuclear power plants, and waste from industry have damaged many stretches of polar coastline.

The Arctic has already suffered, but in 1991, 40 countries agreed to protect Antarctica over the next 50 years. Industry has been limited and tourists can only visit in a few organized groups. It is important that these areas be conserved for future generations to study and enjoy. We can all work to preserve these amazing unspoilt lands so that one day our children can come here and enjoy their own amazing journeys.

One of the few tourist trips allowed in Antarctic waters.

Glossary

colonies	groups of similar things living together
continent	one of the seven large areas of land that make up the world
extinction	when a type of animal or plant dies out and will never live again
food chain	the natural system in which smaller animals get eaten by bigger animals, who get eaten by even bigger animals, and so it goes on
glacier	a large area of slowly moving ice
iceberg	a large piece of ice floating in the sea
isolated	lonely or far away from other things
lair	place where an animal lives or hides
mammals	warm-blooded animals, like humans, that have hair and feed their young on their mother's milk
mate	when a male and female come together to have babies
migrate	to move from one place to another, often to feed or mate
molecule	a very small part of a chemical
North Pole	the most northern part of the Earth
Northern Hemisphere	the northern half of the Earth
pack-ice	sea ice that has been crushed into one big mass
permafrost	a layer of ice in the ground, below the surface of the Earth, that is always frozen and never melts
permanently	always

plankton	tiny animal and plant life that floats or swims in water
pod	a large group of whales living together
porthole	a window in the side of a ship
predator	an animal that hunts, kills and eats other animals
prey	animals that are hunted by predators
radiation	when energy is sent out in strong waves
regurgitate	to eat and swallow then be sick
rodent	a small mammal like a mouse, squirrel or rat
shoal	a large group of the same type of fish
skidoo	a motorbike on skis for travelling on snow and ice
snout	an animal's nose
South Pole	the most southern part of the Earth
Southern Hemisphere	the southern half of the Earth
submersible	an underwater craft used for deep-sea research
tentacle	a long and flexible part of some animals that is used to feel or touch
thaw	when ice or snow melts
thrive	to be healthy and live well
tundra	a treeless area in the Arctic with permafrost, mosses and shrubs
tusk	a big tooth that sticks out of an animal's mouth, even when it is closed

Further reading and addresses

Books

Arctic and Antarctic, Eyewitness Guides series, Barbara Taylor, Dorling Kindersley, 1995

Cold Climates, Keith Lye, Wayland, 1996

Ice-caps and Glaciers, Hands on Geography series, Clint Twist, Gloucester Press, 1992

Nature Cross-sections, Richard Orr, Dorling Kindersley, 1995

Polar Bear and Grizzly Bear, Spot the Difference series, Rod Theodorou and Carole Telford, Heinemann Library, 1996

Polar Bears, Jump! Animal Book series, Lucy Baker, Franklin Watts, 1990

Polar Lands, Ecology Watch series, Rodney Aldis, Evans Brothers, 1991

Polar Wildlife, Usborne World Wildlife series, Kamini Khanduri, Usborne, 1992

Seals and Sea-lions, Wildlife at Risk series, Vassili Papastavrou, Wayland, 1991

Seals, Jump! Animal Book series, Lucy Baker, Franklin Watts, 1990

Wolves, Wildlife at Risk series, Gillian Standing, Wayland, 1991

Organizations

Earthwatch, Belsyre Court, 57 Woodstock Road, Oxford, OX2 6HU, UK

Friends of the Earth, 26-28 Underwood Street, London N1 7JQ, UK,
Tel (0171) 490 1555

Greenpeace, Canonbury Villas, London, N1 2PN, UK, Tel (0171) 354 5100

Marine Conservation Society, 4 Gloucester Road, Ross-on-Wye, Herefordshire,
HR9 5AU, UK

Royal Society for Nature Conservation, The Green, Nettleham, London
LN2 2NR, UK

Waste Watch, National Council for Voluntary Organisations, 26 Bedford Square,
London, WC1B 3HU, UK

Whale and Dolphin Conservation Society, 19A James Street West, Bath, Avon
BA1 2BT, UK

World Wide Fund for Nature, Panda House, Weyside Park, Catteshall Lane,
Godalming, Surrey GU7 1XR, UK, Tel (01483) 426444

Index